DESTINATION FRANCE

Survival Language Course

Part Three

Student's Book

by

D. L. ELLIS
Director, The Language Centre, Taunton

and

M. R. PEARCE
Deputy Head, Benfield Comprehensive School,
Newcastle-upon-Tyne

HARRAP LONDON

Designed by Jonathan Sharp
Produced for the Publishers by
Book Production Consultants, Cambridge

First published in Great Britain 1979
by GEORGE G. HARRAP & CO. LTD.
182–4 High Holborn, London WC1V 7AX

ISBN 0 245 53318 4

Printed in Great Britain by
Billing & Sons Limited
Guildford, London and Worcester

Introduction

With the assistance of your teacher and this book, you will have the opportunity of learning the French you need in the home, with a French friend.

The French you learn will be useful if you go to stay with a friend, or if your friend comes to this country to stay with you. This does not *mean that you will be able to have long conversations in French. It means that you will make life a lot easier for yourself and for the French person you make contact with.*

As well as speaking and listening, there is some reading and writing for you to try your hand at. To help you with the reading, a word list has been prepared, and starts on page 73.
There are also some photographs of the inside of a French house for you to look at and study. Your teacher will explain the things to look out for in these photos.

CONTACT ONE BEING INTRODUCED

Being introduced

How's it done?

Whenever you are being introduced to a French person, you need to know the right things to say and to do. It is not difficult to be polite:

1 Remember always to shake hands with the person to whom you are being introduced.

2 The French handshake is short, and is over in two seconds.

3 Remember to give a person, who is older than you, his or her correct title: **monsieur, madame** or **mademoiselle.**

The dialogue which you are going to learn will be suitable wherever you are being introduced: at an airport, a railway station, a bus terminus, at home, at a party or in the street.

Whom are you likely to meet in the family?

This is how your French friend might tell you who everyone is when you meet them face to face.

Voici mon père (papa)

Voici ma mère (maman)

Voici mon frère

Voici ma sœur

Voici mon grand-père
(papy ou pépé)

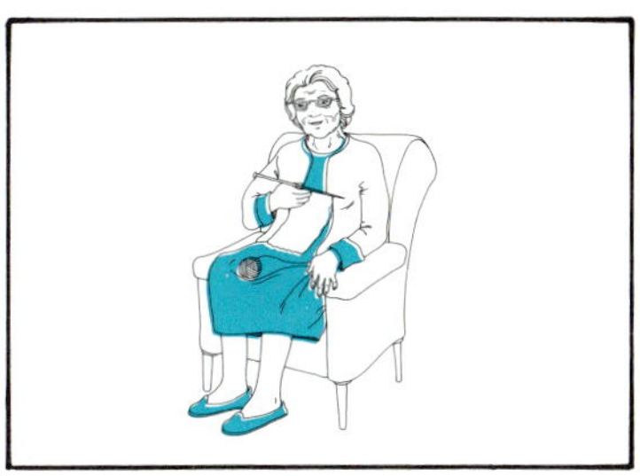

Voici ma grand-mère
(mamie ou mémé)

Model Dialogue 1

In this scene, David has just got off the train, and is recognised by his French friend, Lucien. Lucien's father has brought Lucien to the station to take David to their home.

Model Dialogue 2

In this scene, Angela has just got off the train, and is recognised by her French friend, Yvette. Yvette's mother has brought Yvette to the station to take Angela to their home.

Letter Box

Here are a few lines from the beginning of the letter which Lucien wrote to invite David to come and stay with him. David found the letter quite difficult to read and understand. See how you manage.

> Cher David,
>
> Voici enfin une lettre ! Je t'écris aujourd'hui pour t'inviter à venir passer quinze jours chez moi pendant les grandes vacances. J'espère que tes parents vont dire oui. Réponds vite !
>
> Papa et Maman sont d'accord pour ta visite. Ma sœur va partir chez ma tante italienne en juillet, ainsi tu auras sa chambre. Tu feras la connaissance de toute la famille (mes parents, mon oncle Jacques, mes cousins) et aussi de tous les copains.

1. Do you think Lucien and David write to each other very often?
2. How long is Lucien inviting David to stay?
3. When would be a good time for the visit?
4. Why would that be a good time?
5. Which young people will David get to know?

Puzzle it out!

Here are a few notes about the Jamet family. Work out who's who – and then see if you can answer the questions which follow.

La Famille Jamet

1 Lucien Jamet a un frère (Bernard) et une sœur (Claire).

2 Leurs parents s'appellent François et Henriette.

3 Henriette Jamet est la fille de M. et Mme. Lucas.

4 Elle a une sœur, Brigitte.

5 Le mari de Brigitte est Jacques Aubert.

6 Jacques et sa femme ont une fille Yvette et un fils Georges.

7 Ils sont les cousins de Lucien.

8 Les parents de l'oncle Jacques sont morts.

9 Les grands-parents de Lucien sont M. et Mme. Jamet et M. et Mme. Lucas.

10 Papa a une sœur, Tante Adrienne. Elle n'est pas mariée.

****

1 How many grand-parents has Lucien Jamet?

2 What are the names of his two aunts?

3 How many cousins has Georges Aubert?

4 What are the names of the grand-children of M. and Mme. Lucas?

5 Two members of the Jamet family can be called 'Mademoiselle Jamet'. Who are they?

Let's write!

Read again 'La Famille Jamet' above, and draw up the Jamet family tree. Write in French everyone's name and what relation everyone is to Lucien Jamet. Your teacher can give you a printed sheet to help you, and there are one or two clues on it.

'Je te présente mon grand-père.'

Looking round the House

L'extérieur de la Maison (1)

Voici deux maisons.

Elles sont grandes et belles.

Elles ont deux étages.

1

2

CONTACT TWO SAYING WHICH FOOD AND DRINK Y

Saying which food and drink you like and dislike

les épinards

les haricots

Speak up or eat up

Soon after arrival at a French friend's home, it will be time to sit down for a meal. During your stay, you will probably have a lot of eating to do, so you might as well get things straight at the start.

Rule 1: Remember that most French mothers take a pride in their cooking, and plan meals carefully.

Rule 2: Do not leave food on your plate without saying anything.

Rule 3: Do not be afraid to say that you do not like it.

Rule 4: When you are eating, you can always say that you like something even if you have not been asked. Your friend's mother would take this as a compliment.

You are going to learn

how to say that you do not like something.

how to say that you *do* like something.

how to sound unsure but willing.

How do you feel about these?

le fromage

le pâté

la soupe

la salade

le vin

le Perrier

le cidre

le Banga

LIKE AND DISLIKE

Model Dialogue 1

In this scene, Yvette is looking around the kitchen before the meal, trying to find out what Angela likes and does not like.

Model Dialogue 2

In this scene, Lucien's father is trying to find out what David likes, during the meal. David is a bit lost, but he is willing and manages to keep smiling.

What was that question again?

DO YOU LIKE SALAD?

Here are six different ways a French person might ask you that question.

1 **Tu aimes la salade?**

2 **Est-ce que tu aimes la salade?**

3 **Aimes-tu la salade?**

4 **Vous aimez la salade?**

5 **Est-ce que vous aimez la salade?**

6 **Aimez-vous la salade?**

The ones to learn to say are:

Tu aimes la salade? when you ask someone your own age or younger.
Vous aimez la salade? when you ask an adult, or if you are not sure about someone's age.

The important thing is to make it *sound* like a question.

Just Looking

As you look round a house you will notice that packets, boxes, and bottles have reading on them. In a French house most of the reading will be French. If you are going to get the best out of a short stay in France you will need to be interested in everything and develop a healthy curiosity – without being rude, of course!
In this Contact we are interested in food.

1 Is this a container of (a) salt, (b) fish, or (c) whale meat?

2
Does this box contain a mix for making (a) cakes, (b) batter, or (c) potato?

3
In this packet will you find (a) spaghetti, (b) chicken, or (c) soup mix?

4
In this box will you find (a) cheese, (b) cream, or (c) spinach?

5
Does this box contain (a) chocolates, (b) sugar, or (c) biscuits?

6
Does this carton contain (a) cream, (b) cheese, or (c) cheese spread?

7
In this pot is there (a) milk, (b) yoghurt, or (c) raspberries?

Letter Box

In this extract from a letter written by Yvette to Angela there are some important questions about what people like to eat and drink. Read it carefully and see how much you can understand.

Est-ce que tu aimes les légumes? Moi, j'aime bien les épinards les haricots les pommes de terre et la salade. Georges n'aime pas les carottes.

Qu'est-ce que tu aimes comme fromage en Angleterre? Le Cheddar me plaît beaucoup. Je voudrais essayer le Cottage Cheese. En France tu vas essayer le Camembert, le Bleu de Bresse, et le Brie. Ils sont délicieux, les fromages français.

A table, les parents boivent du vin, du cidre ou de la bière. Mais en général, les enfants boivent du Perrier, du Banga, ou de la limonade par exemple. Qu'est-ce que tu aimes comme boisson? Tu vas certainement essayer un peu de vin. Aimes-tu le thé? Moi, je ne suis pas sûre. Mon frère Georges aime bien le café.

How did you manage?

1 Which vegetables does Yvette like?

2 What does Georges not like?

3 Which English cheese does Yvette like?

4 Which English cheese would Yvette like to try?

5 Which French cheese will Angela be able to try during her visit?

6 What do Yvette's parents generally drink at meal times?

7 What do the children generally drink at meal times?

8 Which of these drinks will Angela be able to try during her visit?

9 Does Yvette like tea?

10 Which drink does Yvette's brother like very much?

Puzzle it out!

One of the first 'adventures' for an English boy or girl in France is to go shopping for the family – and come back with all the right things and the correct change. Read the following imaginary conversation.

On fait les courses

Madame: Ce soir on va manger des escalopes de veau, mais nous n'avons pas de fruits.

You: J'aime bien les raisins.

Madame: Bien. Alors, achetez un kilo de raisins et des poires aussi . . . Un kilo. Et prenez du fromage . . . un Reblochon, peut-être . . . oui, c'est ça, un Reblochon.

You: Où faut-il aller, madame?

Madame: Allez à l'alimentation générale au coin de la rue de la Nuée Bleue. Et n'oubliez pas une bouteille de vin blanc. Achetez une bouteille de Sylvaner. Mon mari aime ça. Voilà cinquante francs.

1 What is the main course planned for the evening meal?

2 What kind of fruit are you going to buy?

3 What else will you buy to eat?

4 Where is the shop? What kind of a shop is it?

5 What sort of drink must you buy?

6 How much money does Madame give you?

Let's write!

Read again 'On fait les courses' on page 15. Imagine that it is your job to do the shopping, and that you are afraid of forgetting what it is you have to ask for. Make out a shopping list in French showing the quantities of all the things you are going to buy as well as their names.

Looking round the House

L'Extérieur de la Maison (2)

Voici la boîte aux lettres.
Elle est dans le jardin, près de la rue.

1

2

Le garage est sous la maison.

Ces maisons sont très vieilles. Elles ne sont pas modernes, mais elles sont belles et intéressantes. Les vieilles maisons sont souvent des magasins, des restaurants, ou des brasseries. Est-ce qu'il y a des volets, ou des balcons, ou des garages? Il n'y a certainement pas de jardins.

3

4

5

CONTACT THREE REFUSING AND ACCEPTING MORE

Refusing and accepting more at meals

Listening for more

You are going to learn a polite way of refusing and accepting more. This is very easy, but the most important thing is to understand when you are being offered more.

What are you being offered?

du pain

du Perrier

du vin

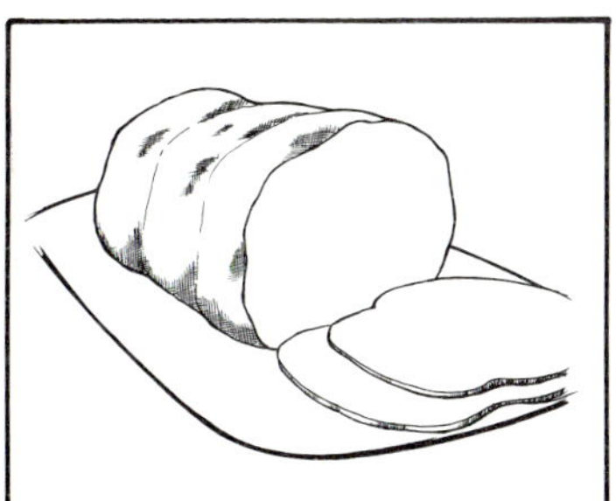

de la viande

de la soupe

de la salade

des pommes de terre

des haricots

des carottes

MEALS

Model Dialogue 1

In this scene, Lucien is asking David if he would like some more.

Model Dialogue 2

In this scene, Yvette's mother is asking Angela if she would like some more.

What was that question again?

WOULD YOU LIKE SOME MORE SALAD?

Here are six different ways a French person might ask you that question.

1 **Tu veux encore de la salade?**

2 **Est-ce que tu veux encore de la salade?**

3 **Veux-tu encore de la salade?**

4 **Vous voulez encore de la salade?**

5 **Est-ce que vous voulez encore de la salade?**

6 **Voulez-vous encore de la salade?**

The ones to learn to say are:

Tu veux encore de la salade? when you ask someone your own age or younger.
Vous voulez encore de la salade? when you ask an adult, or if you are not sure about someone's age.

Just looking

This time you are looking for things to drink, which means reading the labels on the bottles or cans very carefully. After all, not everything in bottles is good to drink.
Read the labels on the bottles in the photographs and see how much you can find out about what they contain.

1

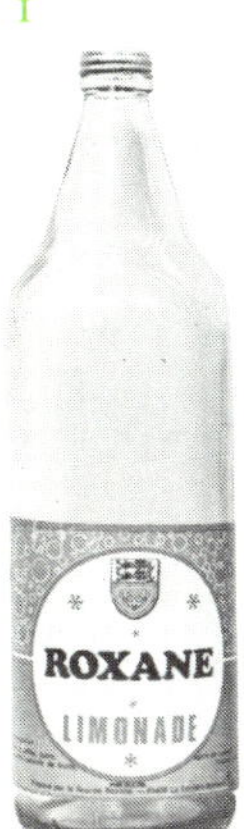

2

3

4

5

Now try these. Which do you think you would prefer to drink? Which would you definitely not drink?

6

7

8

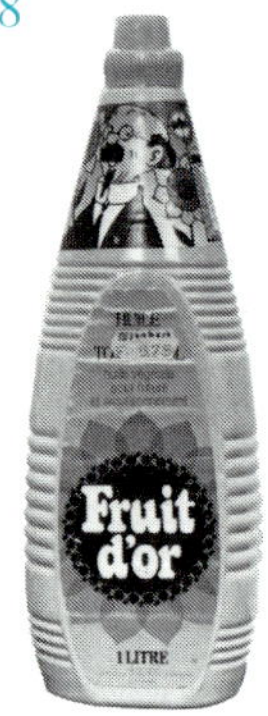

9

10

Puzzle it out!

Today is someone's birthday, and three French teenagers have met in the local café for a little celebration. Read the conversation carefully and try to work out the answers to the questions which follow the conversation.

Au Café
— Bon anniversaire, Jean-François !
— Merci. Tu vas boire à mes 17 ans, Claudine?
— Je veux bien. Un café-crême, s'il te plaît.
— Et toi, Denis? Encore un pamplemousse?
— Non, merci. Cette fois je vais essayer un jus de tomate.
— Un jus de tomate? Tu ne préfères pas un pamplemousse?
— Non, non. C'est trop sucré. Un jus de tomate, s'il te plaît.
— Très bien. Garçon ! Un café-crême, un jus de tomate, et un demi pour moi, s'il vous plaît.

1 Whose birthday is it?

2 Who is having coffee?

3 What does Denis decide to have?

4 Is that his first drink?

5 What does Jean-François do to get the drinks?

6 What does he have himself?

That's not funny!

Let's write!

Imagine that you are in a French cafe with a group of five French friends, perhaps celebrating a birthday. You are all deciding what to have to drink, and it is your job to make a list of what everyone wants. Write down the names of everyone in the group including yourself – you can choose the French names you like – and write in French the name of a drink against each person's name. If you look back at the 'Just looking' and 'Puzzle it out!' sections you should find some helpful ideas.

Looking round the House

La Salle à Manger
Voici la salle à manger.
Regardez la table.
C'est une table ronde.

1

Sur la table il y a
une nappe, une bouteille de vin, une bouteille d'eau minérale, une corbeille de pain, et quatre couverts – assiette, fourchette, couteau, et verre.

2

CONTACT FOUR *IDENTIFYING YOURSELF*

Identifying yourself

Who are you?

You are going to learn how to give your name, age, nationality, and say where you live in this country. This information would be of interest to the friends of your French friend the first time you meet them. They will not *all* know much about you.
You are also going to learn how to ask French people the right sort of questions so that you can find out about them as well.

Model 1

Model 2

What was that question again?

Four questions to remember.
Learn the ones which are underlined. You should only use them for talking to other teenagers and people younger than yourself.

1. **Comment tu t'appelles?** / **Comment t'appelles-tu?** / **Comment vous appelez-vous?** — What is your name?
2. **Tu as quel âge?** / **Quel âge as-tu?** / **Vous avez quel âge?** — How old are you?
3. **Tu es de quelle nationalité?** / **Vous êtes de quelle nationalité?** — What nationality are you?
4. **Tu habites où?** / **Où est-ce que vous habitez?** — Where do you live?

Make sure that you can understand all the questions in French if someone asks you.

Just Looking

You will probably glance at French magazines from time to time and find that they are very much like English ones. You will not want to read them from cover to cover, but it can be fun to dip into them and understand the main points of some articles.
Readers' letters to the problem page often make interesting reading. You sometimes find that other people have similar problems to yours as well.
See how much you can find out about this young French girl's problem.

Chère Marie-Claire,
Je suis très malheureuse. J'ai quinze ans et mon père (mes parents sont divorcés) ne veut jamais me laisser sortir seule le soir à Paris. Je n'ai ni frères ni soeurs, je ne connais pas ma mère, et ma seule vraie amie habite maintenant le centre de Paris. C'est elle qui m'invite de temps en temps dans des discothèques ou au cinéma avec des copains. L'après-midi ça va, mais le soir c'est toujours la même histoire: je n'ai jamais le droit. Les copains rigolent et disent que je suis un bébé. En plus il n'y a rien à faire ici en banlieue et je m'ennuie mortellement. Mais mon père reste inébranlable. Comment faire pour le convaincre que je suis assez grande pour sortir seule le soir?
Julie (une fleur de banlieue)

1. How old is she?
2. Who does she live with?
3. What does her friend invite her to do?
4. What is it that she isn't allowed to do?
5. Where does she live?
6. Why is she fed up?
7. What advice is she seeking?

Some people find a lot of fun in their horoscopes. Try this one – it could be yours.

CAPRICORNE

24 déc. : Vous aurez l'occasion de rencontrer quelqu'un de formidable qui vous fascinera. Grâce à lui vous vous ferez de nombreux copains.

26 déc. : Vous vous apercevrez qu'il y a une certaine incompréhension entre vous et vos parents. La situation sera plutôt explosive, mais patience, vos problèmes s'aplaniront d'eux-mêmes.

29 déc. : Soyez à votre avantage et gardez votre lucidité car cette journée sera importante pour vous. Les astres seront de votre côté.

9-10 janv. : Soyez plus économe. Vous avez plus de succès que jamais, mais gardez la tête froide.

12 janv. : Une grande joie, le 12 janvier à cause d'une réunion qui vous amusera et qui vous donnera la chance de rencontrer des gens formidables.

17 janv. : Grande résistance physique et vous aurez envie de faire du sport, de vous dépenser. N'hésitez pas.

24 Dec.	You will have the opportunity to meet someone. Will he be (a) terrifying, (b) formidable, (c) fantastic?
26 Dec.	You will have problems with your parents. Will you need (a) to avoid impatience, (b) to take a plane, or (c) to explode with rage?
29 Dec.	This could be a good day for you. Should you (a) go on a journey, (b) keep your wits about you, or (c) take advantage of your friends?
9–10 Jan.	Should you try (a) to spend less, (b) to protect yourself, or (c) put up with failure?
12 Jan.	This day could be (a) very unlucky, (b) a lot of fun, or (c) unhappy. Which?
17 Jan.	You may feel like playing some sport. Should you (a) wait for another day, (b) avoid anything too tiring, or (c) have no hesitation?

Letter Box

In this extract from Lucien's first letter he is telling David something about himself and where he lives. You should find this quite easy to understand.

Je m'appelle Lucien Jamet et j'ai quatorze ans. Je suis ton correspondant français. J'habite avec mes parents, mon frère et ma sœur à Cancale. Cancale est une petite ville située au bord de la mer pas loin de Saint-Malo en Bretagne.

Et toi? Je sais que tu t'appelles David Riley, mais quel âge as-tu? Tu es de quelle nationalité? Anglais, Ecossais, Gallois, ou Irlandais? Et tu habites où exactement? Je sais que Manchester est une grande ville. Est-ce que tu habites au centre?

Now that you have read the extract carefully, see if you can answer these questions.

1. How old is Lucien?
2. How many other people are there living in his house?
3. Where do the Jamets live?
4. What kind of a town is it?
5. Whereabouts in France is the town?
6. What does Lucien already know about David?
7. What does he not yet know about him?
8. What does he know about Manchester?

Puzzle it out!

You have already met the names of a few countries in French (what are they?), and the names of the people who live in them (can you remember those?). For example you could say that 'Un Anglais habite en Angleterre'. Here are some more sentences like that one, but the authors are not very bright and have got things a bit mixed up. Puzzle it out and put them right.

1 Les Gallois habitent . . . en Russie.
2 Un Américain habite . . . au Pays-Bas.
3 Un Belge habite . . . au Canada.
4 Les Russes habitent . . . en Belgique.
5 Le Japon est le pays des . . . Allemands.
6 L'Espagne est le pays des . . . Bretons.
7 Les Hollandais habitent . . . au Pays de Galles.
8 L'Allemagne est le pays des . . . Britanniques.
9 La Grèce est le pays des . . . Japonais.
10 Les habitants de la Bretagne sont les . . . Espagnols.
11 Les habitants de la Grande-Bretagne sont les . . . Grecs.
12 Un Canadien habite . . . aux Etats-Unis.

That's not funny!

Looking round the House

Les Chambres
Voici la chambre des parents.
Il y a un grand lit pour deux personnes.

1

Et voici la chambre d'un enfant. A côté du lit on voit un **réveille-matin** et une lampe.

2

CONTACT FIVE TALKING ABOUT YOUR FAMILY

Talking about your family

Who's who

You are going to learn to say how many brothers and sisters you have, and to give their names and ages. If you do not have any brothers or sisters, you will learn how to say so.
You are also going to learn how to say what your parents do for a living.
At the same time you will learn how to ask French people of your own age about their brothers, sisters and parents.

Model Dialogue 1

Model Dialogue 2

What was that question again?

Eight questions to remember. Learn to ask all of them.

1 **Comment il s'appelle?** – What is his name? (One brother)

2 **Comment ils s'appellent?** – What are their names? (More than one brother *and* a mixture of brothers and sisters)

3 **Comment elle s'appelle?** – What is her name? (One sister)

4 **Comment elles s'appellent?** – What are their names? (More than one sister)

5 **Il a quel âge?** – How old is he? (One brother)

6 **Ils ont quel âge?** – How old are they? (More than one brother *and* a mixture of brothers and sisters)

7 **Elle a quel âge?** – How old is she? (One sister)

8 **Elles ont quel âge?** – How old are they? (More than one sister)

Just Looking

Most people are interested in what they eat and drink. The French are very proud of their excellent cooking and you may be able to pick up one or two good ideas if you are staying with a French family. Also, as in England, many magazines and newspapers have a section devoted to food and drink. Here are two examples.

1 Is this a hot or a cold drink?

2 Would you need a large or a small glass for it?

3 Is there any alcohol in it?

4 How many people is this recipe intended to serve?

TONIC DES MONTAGNES

Pour 1 personne : 1 bouteille de coca-cola, 2 cuillerées de rhum blanc, le jus d'un citron, 1 tranche d'orange.

Mettez le rhum dans un verre, versez le coca-cola et le jus de citron. Ajoutez les glaçons et une tranche d'orange.

Lapereau minute

40 MINUTES

Pour 6 personnes :
2 jeunes lapins
30 g de beurre
2 cuillerées à soupe d'huile
2 échalotes
1 citron
1 tablette de bouillon concentré de volaille
persil
sel, poivre
Préparation : 10 mn
Cuisson : 30 mn

Commencez par préparer le bouillon en faisant fondre le concentré de volaille dans 1/4 de litre d'eau. □ Découpez le lapereau en morceaux en le désarticulant pour éviter les petits os. □ Faites chauffer le beurre et l'huile dans une cocotte, mettez les morceaux de lapin à dorer. □ Réduisez le feu, salez, poivrez, ajoutez les échalotes hachées. Laissez cuire à couvert 25 mn environ. □ Au dernier moment, arrosez le lapin avec le jus du citron, donnez encore 2 ou 3 bouillons. □ Retirez les morceaux de lapin, déglacez le fond de la cocotte avec 1 ou 2 cuillerées de bouillon. □ Versez la sauce sur le lapin dressé dans le plat de service chaud, saupoudrez de persil. **Notre conseil :** le temps de cuisson dépend de l'âge des lapins, vérifiez, en cours de cuisson, en piquant les cuisses avec la pointe d'un couteau, elle doit s'y enfoncer sans forcer.

1 What is the main ingredient of this dish?

2 How many people can be served from this recipe?

3 About how long does it take to cook this dish?

4 What kind of utensil do you need for cooking the main part of the dish?

5 How should it be served?

Why not try one of these recipes?

Letter Box

In the letter from which the following extract is taken Yvette is telling Angela something about her family and asking her a few questions as well. Read it carefully and try to understand it.

> Moi, j'ai un frère Georges, mais je n'ai pas de soeur. Georges a dix ans. Et toi, est-ce que tu as des frères et soeurs? Quel âge ont-ils? J'espère que tu n'es pas fille unique!
>
> Que font tes parents? Est-ce qu'ils travaillent tous les deux? Mon père travaille dans un garage. Il est mécano. Ma mère est vendeuse dans une librairie, et elle est ménagère aussi. Elle a donc beaucoup de travail et je lui donne un coup de main de temps en temps. Est-ce que tu travailles à la maison aussi?

How did you manage?

1 Has Yvette any sisters?

2 How old is her brother?

3 What does she hope about Angela?

4 What four things does Yvette want to know?

5 What is Yvette's father's work?

6 What does her mother do?

7 What does Yvette do for her mother?

8 Why does she do this?

Puzzle it out!

You have already learnt the names of a few jobs, such as 'ingénieur', and 'secrétaire'. You cannot possibly learn what all jobs are called in French, so some intelligent guessing is a great help. It is useful to know where people work and what they do there. That helps to get things a little clearer.
Here are some notes about a variety of people and their work. Puzzle them out!

Au Travail

A *Monique* est serveuse dans un restaurant au bord de la mer.

B *Jean-Claude* travaille aux bureaux de la sécurité sociale à Dinan. Il est fonctionnaire.

C *Brigitte* est étudiante à la faculté de médecine. Elle a 20 ans.

D *Bernard* est ouvrier dans une usine. Il n'aime pas son travail et voudrait travailler dehors.

E *Claire* a 25 ans et travaille dans une école primaire. Elle est institutrice. Elle aime bien les enfants.

F *Alain* veut devenir chef de cuisine. Il fait ses études à l'Ecole Hôtelière. Il travaille très dur.

G *Danièle* ne travaille pas – elle cherche un emploi dans un magasin. Son frère est employé de banque.

H *Robert* aussi est sans travail – il attend le service militaire. Son père est retraité et sa mère est femme de chambre dans un hôtel à Saint-Malo.

1 Who has no work?

2 Who is still training for a job?

3 Who has an office job?

4 Who works in a factory?

5 Who works in the hotel and catering trade?

6 Who is a government employee?

That's not funny!

Looking round the House

Le Petit Déjeuner
Voici la table de la cuisine.

1

2

Le petit déjeuner est prêt.
Qu'est-ce qu'on va manger et boire? Pain, beurre, café, 'Banania', gelée de groseilles.

3

Le petit déjeuner est terminé.
On va faire la vaisselle.

CONTACT SIX TALKING ABOUT YOURSELF

Talking about yourself

Mainly school

You will learn how to say:

1 which year group you are in at school.

2 which subject you prefer.

3 which subject you do not like very much.

4 which pastime you like most.

You will learn to understand the questions French people might ask to find out about you.
You will learn to ask French people the right questions to find out about them.
But cheer up. There is more to come.

Model 1

Angela Mackintosh is talking about herself.

Model 2

David Riley is talking about himself.

What was that question again?

1 To find out which year group you are in:
Tu es dans quelle classe à l'école?
Vous êtes dans quelle classe à l'école?

2 To find out which subject you prefer:
Qu'est-ce que tu préfères comme matière?
Qu'est-ce que vous préférez comme matière?

3 To find out which subject you like least:
Qu'est-ce que tu aimes le moins?
Qu'est-ce que vous aimez le moins?

4 To find out which pastime you like:
Qu'est-ce que tu aimes comme distraction?
Qu'est-ce que vous aimez comme distraction?

You should be able to understand all these questions when you hear them. Learn the ones which are underlined.

Just Looking

Sporting events are almost always advertised by posters or large sign-boards like this one. Would you be interested, or able to go?

1 What kind of sporting events are being advertised?

2 How many competitions are there in July?

3 How many days of racing are there in August?

4 Where are the races held?

5 Are the competitions held at the same place?

Perhaps more people are interested in sport – playing or watching – than in any other pastime. It is as true in France as it is in England, and so sport is extensively reported in French newspapers and magazines. You might very well try to read a bit about your favourite sport and be surprised to find how many of the words you can recognise. Try these two short pieces.

CAEN : BASSE-NORMANDIE

CYCLO-CROSS

Pendant les mois d'hiver, certains coureurs cyclistes poursuivent leur entraînement en pratiquant ce sport.

NANTES : PAYS DE LOIRE

PATINS A ROULETTES

Initiation à ce jeu qui peut devenir un sport de compétition.

FOOTBALL

Portrait de **Raymond Keruzore.**

POITIERS : POITOU-CHARENTES

LES RALLYES AUTOMOBILES

A qui sont-ils ouverts, hormis les professionnels de la compétition automobile ?

RENNES : BRETAGNE

NATATION

Troisième volet sur la pratique de ce sport en Bretagne.

ROUEN : HAUTE-NORMANDIE

BILAN ET ESPOIRS

Rétrospective sportive avec le cycliste **Raymond Delisle,** l'équipe de handball de Gonfreville-l'Orcher et les athlètes régionaux sélectionnés pour Montréal.

There are eight sports mentioned directly or indirectly here. What are they?

Basket

Championnat : un péril pour Berck

Un seul match entre équipes de premier plan ce soir (20 h 45) : Antibes-Berck. Un risque sérieux pour les Nordistes de perdre leur 3ᵉ place. Villeurbanne (1ᵉʳ), Caen (2ᵉ) et Le Mans (4ᵉ) seront moins inquiets : leurs visiteurs sont tous en mauvaise posture.

Deuxième tour-retour. — Tours-Stade Français ; Villeurbanne-Tarare ; Antibes-Berck ; Le Mans-Valenciennes ; Bagnolet - Challans, à Coubertin ; Caen - Lyon ; Clermont - Nice ; Monaco-Orthez.

Berck is a small seaside resort, but has a very good team for a certain sport. Which sport? What is the danger for Berck in this evening's match?

Letter Box

In this letter Lucien is talking about himself again. This time he is telling David about school and what he likes doing in his spare time. He is also asking about David.

Tu es dans quelle classe à l'école ? Moi je suis en troisième. Je trouve que nous avons beaucoup de travail. Je préfère les maths, la physique et la chimie, mais je n'aime pas tellement l'histoire. Notre prof d'histoire est très sévère. Et toi, qu'est-ce que tu préfères comme matière, et qu'est-ce que tu aimes le moins ?

Comme distraction j'aime surtout la musique et j'ai beaucoup de disques. J'aime aller aux concerts pour écouter les groupes. J'aime aussi le basket et le hand-ball. Est-ce que tu aimes le sport ? Tu joues sans doute au football à l'école.

What did you learn about Lucien?

1. Which class is Lucien in?
2. Which year of secondary school is that in France?
3. Does he think he has an easy time in school?
4. What are his favourite school subjects?
5. Which does he like least? Why?
6. What does he like doing for relaxation?
7. What sports does he play?
8. What sport does he expect David to play?

Puzzle it out!

Here is the timetable for a French pupil in 'troisième'. Study it carefully and compare it with your own timetable. There are some questions for you to answer. Answer for yourself and your timetable as well as for the French pupil.

	Lundi	Mardi	Mercredi	Jeudi	Vendredi	Samedi
8H à 9H	maths	lecture, expliquée		anglais	E.P.S	technologie
9H à 10H	permanence	histoire		allemand	E.P.S	technologie
10H à 11H	orthographe	latin		maths	latin	anglais
11H à 12H	lecture suivie	grammaire		instruction civique	allemand	latin
14H à 15H	anglais	géographie		sciences naturelles	allemand	
15H à 16H	dessin	latin		maths (classe dédoublée)	français	
16H à 17H	travaux manuels	maths			musique	

1 At what time do lessons start in the morning?

2 When do they finish in the afternoon?

3 What meal times and breaks are there?

4 Which days are school days?

5 How long do lessons last?

6 How long is spent on lessons in a full week?

7 How much time is given to the different subjects?

8 Which subjects are not included in the French timetable that you might have expected to find?

That's not funny!

Let's write

Imagine that you have to fill in a form in French. You are required to give details about yourself, and the information is asked for under the following headings:

1. NOM
2. ADRESSE
3. AGE
4. DATE DE NAISSANCE
5. ÉCOLE & CLASSE
6. MATIÈRES PRÉFÉRÉES
7. DISTRACTIONS PRÉFÉRÉES
8. MÉTIER/PROFESSION ENVISAGÉ

Draw up and complete the form.

Alternatively

Try to write a short letter in French about yourself and your family. Look at the letters in the Letter Box sections of Contacts 4, 5 and 6. Try to imitate the way Lucien and Yvette express themselves.

Looking round the House

La Cuisine (1)

1

Voici l'évier. L'évier est dans la cuisine. Il y a un seul robinet pour l'eau chaude et l'eau froide.

2

La vaisselle est faite. Sur l'évier on voit deux casseroles, des tasses à café, des soucoupes, et des cuillers.

3

Dans la cuisine on trouve des produits de ménage.
Il ne faut pas les boire! Voici:
de l'eau de Javel pour désinfecter,
'Carolin' pour nettoyer les carrelages,
'PPZ' pour nettoyer les tapis,
'Décap Four' pour nettoyer l'intérieur de la cuisinière,
et 'Harpic' pour nettoyer le W.C., comme en Angleterre.
Remarquez le white spirit 'Spirdane'.

CONTACT SEVEN ASKING PERMISSION

Asking permission

May I?

If you are staying in a strange house, you may not be sure how to behave at times. To be on the safe side, always ask permission when you want to do something that might disturb others.
You are going to learn a polite way of asking permission. You are also going to learn to understand some of the answers you might hear.

Some of the things you might want to do

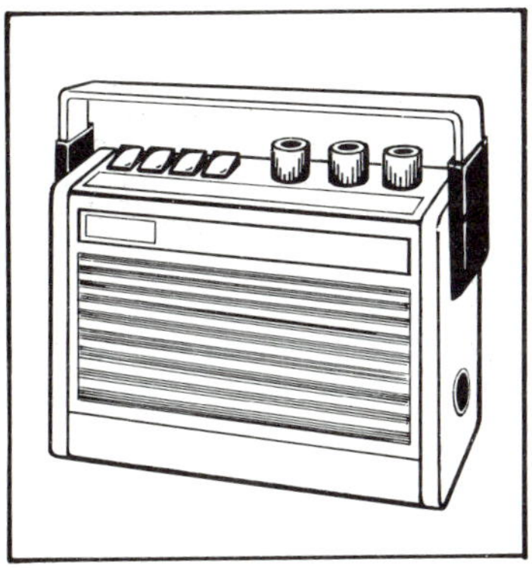

(écouter) la radio

(regarder) la télévision

(prendre) un thé

(écouter) des disques

(regarder) des illustrés

(prendre) une douche

Model Dialogue 1

In this scene, Angela is asking Yvette's permission to watch television.

Model Dialogue 2

In this scene, David is asking Lucien if he may have a cup of tea.

What was that again?

You ask for permission to do something. But can you understand the answer? It may not be a straight YES or NO.

OUI	NON
Bien sûr.	**Je suis désolé(e).**
Fais comme chez toi.	**Certainement pas.**
Si tu veux.	**Je regrette.**
Sers-toi.	**Ce n'est pas possible.**
Vas-y.	**Attends.**

But that is not the end of it. There are plenty of other ways of saying YES and NO. Listen to the voice, and watch the face of the person speaking. You will learn a lot that way.

Just Looking

It is almost certain that you would want to watch television or listen to the radio in France and you may well need to look in the newspaper or in a special magazine such as 'Télérama' to find out what is on. There are three television channels, and on radio the main stations are France-Musique, France-Culture, and France-Inter. In addition one can usually receive programmes from Europe I, Belgique I, Monte-Carlo, R.T.L. (Luxembourg) and Sottens (Switzerland) at least.

Here are some programme details. See what you can understand.

France-Culture O.M.

5.30 Emissions pour les travailleurs étrangers : **5.30** Portugais ; **5.55** Arabes ; **6.20** Turcs ; **6.30** Yougoslaves ; **6.40** Espagnols ; **6.50** Italiens.

7. Le réveil musculaire, par Robert Raynaud. — **7.15** Pour PARIS : **France-Culture M.F. ;** Pour la PROVINCE : **Emissions régionales.**

8. France-Culture : Voir M.F.

9. Radio scolaire : Initiation musicale.

9.15 à 14. France-Culture : voir M.F. (sauf pour la PROVINCE, de **12.5** à **12.30 Emissions régionales).**

14. à 18. Radio scolaire : 14. Vie contemporaine ; **14.20 Allemand** (quatrième) ; **14.40 Anglais** (quatrième) ; **15. Allemand** (troisième) ; **15.20** Que se passe-t-il ici ? ; **15.35** Initiation à la poésie ; **15.50** Disques ; **17.** Information des professeurs : Français et Pédagogie.

18. Emissions universitaires jusqu'à **19.** (en province) et **20.** (à Paris). Ensuite : **France-Culture** : voir M.F. **24.** Fin.

1 At what time would you listen to schools radio for a programme of English?

2 What would be on this station at 6.30 pm?

3 At what time could you hear a programme in Italian for migrant workers?

12.15 à 18.30 RELAIS DE TF 1

18.45 POUR LA JEUNESSE

FLASH. « **A quoi bon la musique** », avec les élèves du C.E.S. Joliot-Curie d'Amiens. (Emis. d'Hélène Fatou. Réal. : Fernand Vincent. Une production de Lille.)

19.5 MAGAZINES REGIONAUX

AMIENS. **Boxe** : Portrait du professionnel Robert Amory, de Compiègne, qui va affronter en finale du Championnat de France des mi-lourds l'Ardennais Christian Poncelet.

NANTES. **Handball et football.** Deux sections « Sport-Etudes » créées dans l'académie de Nantes à la rentrée dernière.

LIMOGES. **Football.** Le Cercle Saint-Pierre face à son destin... et au Racing, table ronde.

POITIERS. **Spéléologie,** reportage (sans précisions).

NICE. **Ski.** Avec les jeunes de la Ligue française de l'Enseignement.

BESANÇON. **Hockey sur glace.** Initiation des enfants à la compétition.

ROUEN. **Sports de glace.** Leur pratique par grands et petits en Haute-Normandie.

ORLEANS. **Un sport en flèche : le tir à l'arc.** Redevenu discipline olympique il y a cinq ans.

STRASBOURG, NANCY, REIMS, LILLE, RENNES, BORDEAUX, TOULOUSE, MONTPELLIER, MARSEILLE, LYON, DIJON, CLERMONT-FERRAND, PARIS et CAEN présentent leurs magazines sportifs respectifs (sans précisions).

19.20 ACTUALITES REGIONALES

19.40 TRIBUNE LIBRE

Emission de Jean-Pierre Alessandri et Jean-Claude Michelot.

Louis Pauwels : l'anti-sinistrose. Cet auteur entend lutter contre le sentiment de culpabilité et de découragement de l'occident. D'après lui, les terreurs de l'an 2000 ne sont que les erreurs de l'an 2000. Son principal cheval de bataille est une attaque contre ce qu'il appelle les mythes créés par le club de Rome, mythes concernant la surpopulation, la famine et l'épuisement des ressources naturelles. Il conseille

1 There is a programme especially for young people at 18.45. What is the topic?

2 After that what could you watch if you were in the area of (a) Besançon, (b) Orléans, or (c) Amiens?

3 At what time are the regional news programmes shown?

Look carefully at these notes about some of the television programmes being shown during one week. See how much you can understand, and when you have puzzled it out have a go at the questions.

NOTEZ POUR LA SEMAINE DU 15 AU 21 JANVIER

TELEVISION FRANÇAISE 1

SAMEDI 15 : 20.30 Numéro Un, Eddy Mitchell. 21.30 Chapeau melon et bottes de cuir. — DIMANCHE 16 : 20.30 Les Seins de glace. 22. Questionnaire, Vassili Leontiev. — LUNDI 17 : 20.30 A bout de souffle, film de Jean-Luc Godard. 22. Portrait, Fritz Lang. — MARDI 18 : 22. Le livre du mois. — MERCREDI 19 : 20.30 La foire, film T.V. de Pierre Viallet (1). 22. Les grandes énigmes, la Soufrière. — JEUDI 20 : 20.30 La Famille Cigale, feuilleton de G. Sire (2). 22. L'Evénement. — VENDREDI 21 : 20.30 Mademoiselle Julie, pièce de A. Strindberg. 22.15 Arcana, Les femmes et la musique.

ANTENNE 2

SAMEDI 15 : Les beaux messieurs de Bois-Doré (5), d'après G. Sand. 22. Questions sans visages, de Pierre Dumayet. — DIMANCHE 16 : 13.25 Le dimanche de Jacques Martin. 21.30 Rush. 22.30 Le musée imaginaire, de Michel Butor. — LUNDI 17 : 20.30 La tête et les jambes. 21.55 Gaston Bonheur. 22.50 L'huile sur le feu : le logement en France. — MARDI 18 : Les dossiers de l'écran : Pour l'exemple. — MERCREDI 19 : 20.30 Switch (4). 21.30 C'est à dire. 23. Jazz. — JEUDI 20 : Le silencieux, de Claude Pinoteau. 22.00 Magazine du cinéma. — VENDREDI 21 : 20.30 Dossiers : danger immédiat (1). 21.30 Apostrophes, histoire, actualité et sémiologie du livre cochon. 22.47 Ciné-club : Les joyeux garçons, film de Grégori Alexandrov.

FRANCE REGIONS 3

SAMEDI 15 : 20.30 L'homme en fuite, de Donald Siegel, film TV. — DIMANCHE 16 : 17.50 Espace musical. 20.30 L'homme en question : Jacques Faizant. 22.30 Aventures en Birmanie, de Raoul Walsh. — LUNDI 17 : 20.30 La nuit des généraux, film d'Anatole Litvak. — MARDI 18 : 20.30 Chino, film de John Sturges. — MERCREDI 19 : 20.30 Juste avant la nuit, film de Claude Chabrol. — JEUDI 20 : 20.30 Le Mépris, film de Jean-Luc Godard. — VENDREDI 21 : 21.20 Voyages dans le cosmos, de J. Lallier et M. Tosello.

1 Which week exactly do these notes refer to?

2 What are the names of the three TV channels in France?

3 Which channel should you switch to for a film on Monday evening? Is there a choice?

4 You would like to watch a programme of jazz. Which day, time and channel do you need to switch on?

5 Which channel should you watch for a programme on the cinema? When is it?

Puzzle it out!

When there are several people in a family it is usually necessary to try to fit in with each other's wishes. This is especially true when one of the people is a stranger who might not understand very well if what he wants to do will be acceptable or not. Here are some of the Jamet family talking about what they would like to do. Puzzle out who fits in and who does not.

Chez les Jamet

Lucien: J'ai fini mes devoirs maman. Est-ce que je peux regarder la télé? Il y a un bon film.

Madame: Ah, mon garçon . . . toujours la télé! Mais j'ai mal à la tête ce soir. Tu ne peux pas lire?

Lucien: Si tu veux. Je peux lire ton livre, Claire?

Claire: Vas-y, j'ai fini de le lire. Maman, il y a de l'eau chaude? Je peux prendre une douche?

Madame: Bien sûr, ma fille. Ah, voici Bernard qui arrive.

Bernard: Je peux sortir, maman, avec Henri Lenoir?

Maman: Où veux-tu aller à cette heure? Il est déjà dix heures.

Bernard: On va chez Marcel écouter son nouveau disque. Tu dis oui?

Madame: Je regrette, Bernard, mais il est trop tard. Tu peux écouter le disque un autre jour.

Bernard: Oh, maman! Je ne suis pas un bébé, quand même. Je peux y aller, n'est-ce pas? Il faut une heure au maximum.

Madame: Certainement pas, Bernard. N'en parlons plus.

1 What does Lucien ask to be allowed to do?

2 Why does his mother say no?

3 What does he ask to do instead?

4 Is Claire given permission to do what she wants?

5 What objection does Madame Jamet have to Bernard's wishes?

6 Does Bernard get his own way in the end?

Let's write

Imagine that you are a TV fanatic and that you are going to watch every night of the week. However you like to plan your viewing, and you will need to fit in with the other people in the house.

Look again at the programmes shown in the notes in 'Just Looking' on pp. 46/47. Write in French so that everyone else in the house can understand and make a list of your proposed programmes. Starting on the left of a sheet of paper, put the day, date, time, channel and finally the name of the actual programme.
Set out your plans for the full week. You will want to watch at least one programme each evening. You will of course need to ask permission.

Looking round the House

La Cuisine (2)

Voici la cuisinière.
C'est une cuisinière à gaz.
Maintenant la cuisinière est fermée.

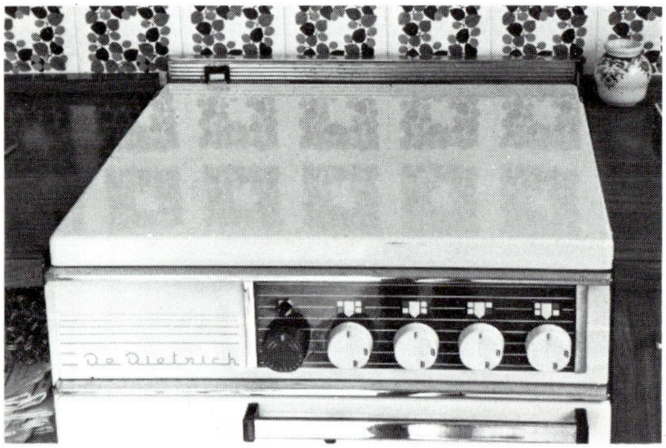

2

1

That's not funny!

CONTACT EIGHT DECIDING WHAT TO DO

On fait
une promenade?

On fait
des achats?

Deciding what to do

It's up to you

Your French friend asks you to suggest something to do, and it's up to you to think of an idea. Then you have to understand whether your friend agrees or disagrees with your suggestion.

Things to do

Of all the things you might want to do, here are eight ideas for you to suggest.

On joue
aux cartes?

On joue
aux boules?

On regarde
la télévision?

On regarde
des illustrés?

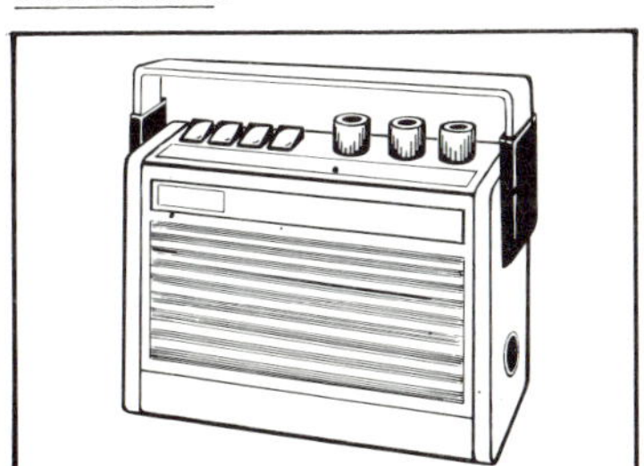

On écoute
la radio?

On écoute
des disques?

Model Dialogue 1

In this scene, Yvette is asking Angela to suggest something to do, and she agrees with Angela's idea.

Model Dialogue 2

In this scene, Lucien is asking David to suggest something to do, but he disagrees with David's idea.

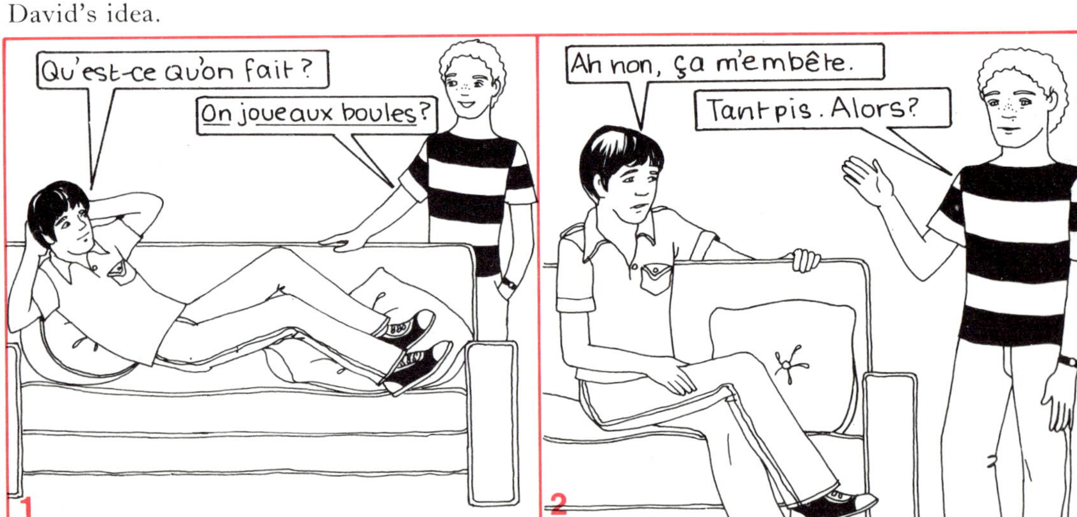

What was that question again?

These four questions in French mean: What do you want to do?

1 **Que veux-tu faire?** – Someone about your own age is asking you.
2 **Que voulez-vous faire?** – Someone older than you is asking you.
3 **Qu'est-ce que tu veux faire?** – Someone about your own age is asking you.
4 **Qu'est-ce que vous voulez faire?** – Someone older than you is asking you.

You must understand these questions when people are speaking to you, but you can always use the one you have learnt when you ask them: **Qu'est-ce qu'on fait?**

What was that again?

FOR and	AGAINST
Bon d'accord. (underlined)	**Ah non, ça m'embête.** (underlined)
Bonne idée.	**Non, c'est ennuyeux.**
Allons-y.	**Ça ne me dit rien.**
Bon, si tu veux.	**Je ne veux pas.**
Très bien.	
Vas-y.	

You must know when people are FOR and AGAINST. Learn the two lists so that you can understand the meaning when you hear them. You should be able to say the two expressions which are underlined.

That's not funny!

Just Looking

A glance at a newspaper can often help you to decide what you would like to do. Details of local cinemas, theatres and concert halls are to be found in French newspapers just as they are in English ones. Here are some cuttings from papers for you to look at.

SPECTACLE SAUNDERS
Comédies anglaises
Avec
Katharina Renn
Odile Mallet
Anne Carrère
Josette Harmina
Robert Murzeau

Anne Carrère

Théâtre Daniel-Sorano
64, rue du Rocher
T.l.s. 20 h 30 sf jeu.
Mat. dim. 14 h 30
522-08-40
Mat. dim. 15 heures
Places à 26 F

1 What kind of plays are being performed?

2 What is the name of the theatre?

3 Where is the theatre?

4 What days is it open in the evenings?

5 What time do evening performances start?

6 What seats are still available?

CASABLANCA
de Michel Curtiz
Aventures
Américain
Noir et blanc
Avec
Humphrey Bogart
Ingrid Bergman
Sydney Greenstreet
Peter Lorre
Claude Rains
Paul Henreid

Humphrey Bogart

Balzac
(v.o.) 359-52-70
Bonaparte
(v.o.) 326-12-12
Action République
(v.o.) 805-51-33
Cujas
(v.o.) 033-89-22
Max Linder
(v.f.) 770-40-04

1 Is the film in colour or black and white?

2 Is the film English, French or American?

3 At which cinemas is it showing?

4 If you wanted to hear the original sound-track, which cinema would you *not* go to?

CALENDRIER DES CONCERTS

Jacques LEBLANC/Guy JOLIE (Belgique)

DATE	GROUPES	VILLE	SALLE	PRIX
17 oct.	ROLLING STONES/ BILLY PRESTON/ KRACKER	Bruxelles	Forest National	28 F
19 oct.	TREMPLIN 505	Paris	Golf Drouot	16,50 F
20 oct.	NOVALIS	Paris	Golf Drouot	16,50 F
	ZAO	Avignon	Théâtre du Chêne Noir	
	GLADY	Vesdun (18)	Foyer Rural	12 F
	VIRUS	Sains-en-Gohelle		
	TITANIC	Seltz	Salle du Cygne	10 F
21 oct.	NOVALIS	Paris	Golf Drouot	16,50 F
	GONG	Porte de Pantin	Théâtre Présent	10 F
23 oct.	ZAO	Rodez	Maison des Jeunes	
24 oct.	COUNTRY GAZETTE/ DERROLL ADAMS	Bruxelles	Beurschouwburg	
	ZAO	Albi	Théâtre Municipal	
25 oct.	SLADE	Bruxelles	Forest National	
	ZAO	Toulouse		
26 oct.	AFTER LIFE	Paris	Golf Drouot	16,50 F
	SLADE	Courtrai		
	STATUS QUO/ ATLANTIS/ALEX HARVEY BAND	Bruxelles	Salle Marni	
27 oct.	VENUS SYSTEME	Paris	Golf Drouot	16,50 F
	STATUS QUO/ MANFRED MANN	Paris	Olympia	
	ATOLL	Hirson	Club l'Interdit	
	GLADY	Ambrault (36)	Apollo 73	12 F
	AFTER LIFE	Paris	Salle Wagram	
28 oct.	VENUS SYSTEME	Paris	Golft Drouot	16,50 F
	SHIRLEY BASSEY	Bruxelles	Palais des Beaux-Arts	
	AFTER LIFE	Epinouze		

1 Where and when could you see and hear the Rolling Stones?

2 What does it cost to go to a concert at Golf Drouot?

3 Which concert halls in Paris are mentioned?

4 Who is playing at the Paris Olympia? When?

Letter Box

In one of his letters Lucien was trying to find out what kind of things David might enjoy doing during his stay in France. This is part of what he wrote.

> Qu'est-ce que tu veux faire pendant ton séjour ? Comme tu le sais, j'aime bien écouter des disques. Je regarde la télévision aussi quand il fait mauvais. Est-ce que tu voudrais jouer aux boules, ou faire des promenades en vélo ? En France beaucoup de gens vont à la pêche. Est-ce que tu aimes la pêche ?
>
> Moi je n'aime pas faire les achats – c'est ennuyeux, n'est-ce pas ? Mon frère aime beaucoup jouer aux cartes, mais ça ne me dit rien. Ma sœur passe des heures à regarder des illustrés et à écouter la radio dans sa chambre.

1 What two things does Lucien particularly like doing?

2 What two things does he suggest David might like to do?

3 What activity is very popular in France?

4 What does Lucien dislike particularly?

5 What does his brother enjoy?

6 What does Lucien think of his brother's pastime?

7 How does his sister spend a lot of her spare time?

Puzzle it out!

Deciding what to do is something that can take quite a lot of discussion when there are several people involved. For you it might not be easy to follow the various suggestions and arguments. See now how you get on with puzzling out the following conversation.

'Qu'est-ce qu'on fait?'

Bernard:	Alors, qu'est-ce qu'on fait cet après-midi?
Yves:	Je ne sais pas, moi. Que veux-tu faire, toi?
Bernard:	On fait une promenade en vélo?
Marie-Claude:	Ah non ! Ça ne me dit rien. Et il fait chaud.
Chantale:	C'est vrai. On peut écouter des disques.
Yves:	Je préfère jouer aux cartes.
Bernard:	D'accord, moi aussi.
Chantale:	Mais on ne fait que ça. Ça m'embête !
Marie-Claude:	Il y a un bon film au ciné.
Chantale:	Mais on va au cinéma ce soir. C'est déjà décidé.
Yves:	Et demain on va au concert. Moi, je vais jouer de la guitare. Voilà !
Bernard:	Bon, si tu veux. Je vais chercher la mienne.
Marie-Claude:	Dans ce cas-là, Chantale, on va écouter des disques, nous.
Chantale:	D'accord !
Yves:	Mais vous allez nous casser les oreilles avec vos disques.
Chantale:	Tant pis pour vous, mes amis !

1 Who wants to go out?

2 Why does Marie-Claude not want to do anything energetic?

3 Why do they decide not to go to the cinema this afternoon?

4 What do the boys decide to do?

5 What do the girls decide to do?

6 What do the boys think of the girls' decision?

7 Who finally does what he or she suggested in the first place?

Let's write

Imagine that you are trying to decide what to do one day and there are eight of you in the group. In order to arrive at a fair decision you agree to put all suggestions in a hat and do whatever comes out first.
You are chosen to write down all the suggestions. Make a list of eight different activities that you might consider for a fine day when everyone wants to be out of doors.
Then do the same again for a rainy day when you all want to be under cover somewhere.
If you revise this Contact you should find enough ideas, but there are even more in Contacts 6, 7 and 9.

Looking round the House

Le Cabinet de Toilette

Dans le cabinet de toilette il y a un lavabo. On voit aussi des serviettes, des brosses à dents, et une glace (un miroir).

1

Dans le coin il y a une douche. Est-ce qu'il y a une baignoire aussi?

2

3

Il y a aussi un bidet.

CONTACT NINE *DECIDING WHERE TO GO*

à la plage

à la campagne

Deciding where to go

The conversation

Your French friend asks if you want to go out.
You say that you do.
Your friend asks you to suggest somewhere.
You suggest a place.
Your friend either agrees or disagrees.

Places to go

Here are eight places where you might want to go.

Three other things to listen for

- several ways of asking: 'Do you want to go out?'
- several ways of agreeing and disagreeing with a suggestion.
- the words for 'this morning', 'this afternoon', 'this evening', 'today' and 'tomorrow'.

à la piscine

en ville

au musée

au café

au cinéma

au stade

Model Dialogue 1

In this scene, Lucien and David are deciding where to go, and Lucien agrees with David's suggestion.

Model Dialogue 2

In this scene, Yvette and Angela are deciding where to go, but Yvette disagrees with Angela's suggestion.

What was that again?

1 Do you want to go out?

Tu veux sortir?
Est-ce que tu veux sortir?
Veux-tu sortir?
On sort?
Est-ce qu'on sort?

2 Agreeing and disagreeing.

Agreeing: **d'accord**, **bonne idée**, **si tu veux**, **très bien**

Disagreeing: **ça m'embête**, **c'est ennuyeux**, **ça ne me dit rien**, **je ne veux pas**

3

ce matin	this morning
cet après-midi	this afternoon
ce soir	this evening
aujourd'hui	today
demain	tomorrow

The words which are underlined are the ones you should be able to say. All the rest, you should be able to understand when you hear them.

Just Looking

If you are looking at the newspaper and thinking about what to do or where to go, the weather forecast is likely to be of some interest. To help you find it, or any other section of a paper or magazine, there is usually a list of contents showing which pages different articles or items are on. Here are three examples for you to look at.

1

On which pages would you find articles or information on (a) news of England, (b) weather forecast, (c) radio and TV programmes, (d) sport, (e) cars, and (f) cinema programmes?

sommaire

Arts **(17)**
Automobile **(12)**
Bourse de Paris **(10)**
Carnet du jour **(18)**
Chronique **(24)**
Courses **(13)**
Economie **(6 à 10)**
Education **(4)**
Equipement **(4)**
Etranger **(2)**
Feuilleton **(8)**
Informations générales **(6)**
Journée **(18)**
Littéraire **(15 à 17)**
Météorologie **(14)**
Mots croisés **(18)**
Philatélie **(13)**
Politique **(2 à 4)**
Programmes spectacles **(22)**
Programmes radio-télévision **(19, 20, 23)**
Religions **(6)**
Social **(4)**
Spectacles **(21)**
Sports **(14)**
Télevision, radio **(22)**

2 Find out as much as you can about the weather forecast for Paris, and then for another region of your own choice.

En France aujourd'hui

REGION PARISIENNE. Brumeux le matin, puis nuageux avec éclaircies l'après-midi. Vent de nord faible. Températures matinales de 0° à 2°, maximales 4° à 5°.

AILLEURS. Sur la plus grande partie du pays, formations brumeuses abondantes et localement denses. Les brouillards (localement givrants dans le Centre) se dissiperont en fin de matinée et on observera quelques éclaircies plus marquées dans l'Ouest. En revanche, de la Flandre à l'Alsace et au nord des Alpes, ciel très nuageux à couvert avec quelques faibles chutes de pluies ou de neige.

Sur la Corse et les régions méditerranéennes, amélioration progressive après une matinée très nuageuse.

Au lever du jour, gelées de l'ordre de 0° à — 3° dans l'intérieur.

PRESSION ATMOSPHERIQUE à Paris le 7 janvier, à 13 heures : 772 millimètres de mercure, soit 1.038 millibars.

RENSEIGNEMENTS ASTRONOMIQUES pour le 8 janvier (exprimés en heure légale française, base d'observation Paris) :

SOLEIL : lever, 8,45 ; pass. au méridien, 12 h 57 ; coucher, 17 h 10 ; durée du jour, 8 h 25.

LUNE (19e jour) : lever, 20 h 58 ; pass. au méridien, 2 h 57 ; coucher, 9 h 24.

Jour julien à 13 heures : 2443152.

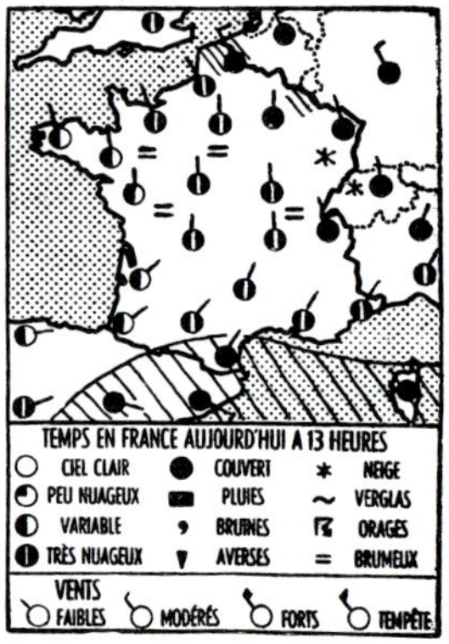

Comme chaque semaine

P. 16 • Livres.
P. 18 • Société
P. 31
et 125 • Cuisine : quatre recettes-fiches
P. 39 • Mots croisés.
P. 46 • ELLE-Club.
P. 57 • Courrier du cœur.
P. 61 • Façons de parler.
P. 92 • Horoscope.
P. 94 • Courrier.
P. 111 • Nos menus.
P. 129 • Basses calories.
P. 131 • Restaurant.
P. 144 • Cinéma.
P. 146 • Entendre et voir.
P. 150 • Voyage.
P. 154 • Tarifs et bulletin d'abonnement.

3 On which pages would you find articles or items on
(a) cookery
(b) slimming diets
(c) films
(d) travel
(e) readers' letters?

Letter Box

Yvette wrote to Angela one day when she was trying to plan outings. She wanted to know the kind of places Angela might like to go during her stay in France.

J'espère que tu aimes bien sortir. Ça m'embête de rester à la maison quand il fait beau. Mon frère va souvent au stade pour regarder les matchs de football – ce n'est pas intéressant pour moi. Est-ce que tu aimes regarder le football?

Si on sort, on peut aller à la plage ou à la campagne, mais on peut aussi aller en ville si tu préfères. Quand je vais en ville avec Maman, c'est toujours pour aller à la poste ou au marché. Avec toi, on peut aller au café ou au cinéma si tu veux. D'accord? Est-ce que tu aimes faire des pique-niques?

1 Does Yvette like to go out?

2 Does she often go out with her brother, do you think?

3 Where does he go, and why?

4 When Yvette goes into town with her mother where do they usually go?

5 Whereabouts in town would Yvette prefer to go with Angela?

6 Where else does Yvette suggest that they might go instead of into town?

Puzzle it out!

Discussions about where to go can be particularly difficult for a person who is a stranger to the area and does not know what the possibilities are. It will help of course if you can let people know the kind of places you like or need to go to, and if you can understand their suggestions and show what your preferences are.
Puzzle out the following discussion.

'Où va-t-on?'

Marc: Eh bien, il fait beau ce matin. On sort?
Adrian: Je veux bien. On va où?
Marc: D'abord il faut aller à la poste, mais après on va où on veut. Si on allait au musée?
Adrian: Les musées sont ennuyeux.
Marc: Tu trouves? A la plage, alors?
Adrian: Mais il y a toujours beaucoup de monde.
Marc: C'est vrai. Alors à la piscine?
Adrian: Je n'aime pas beaucoup la natation.
Marc: Si on allait faire une promenade sur les falaises? Il y a beaucoup à voir. On peut aller jusqu'aux parcs à huîtres.
Adrian: C'est loin?
Marc: Non, non. Trois kilomètres peut-être, quatre au plus.
Adrian: Très bien. Tu as des jumelles?
Marc: Oui, mon père en a. Comme ça on peut regarder les bateaux et les oiseaux, n'est-ce pas?
Adrian: Les oiseaux m'intéressent beaucoup.

1 Where does Marc have to go first of all?
2 What does Adrian think about museums?
3 Why does Adrian not want to go to the beach?
4 Is Adrian a keen swimmer?
5 What does Marc finally propose?
6 How far will they walk?
7 What three things in particular can they look at?
8 What will they need to take with them?

Let's write

Imagine that you are keeping a diary of what you do and where you go during your fortnight's stay in France. You would probably keep it in English, but you are keen to write some bits of it in French just to show yourself and other people that you *can* do it.
Set out the days in a fortnight down the left side of a piece of paper, and opposite each day write down briefly in French the places you went and what you did. Use your imagination and revise this Contact. Contacts 6, 7 and 8 will help as well. Only write what you know. It is not necessary to write full sentences.

That's not funny!

Looking round the House

Les Fenêtres

Voici deux fenêtres.
Il n'y a pas de volets.

1

2

Voici la porte-fenêtre.
On voit le store qui descend pour fermer la porte-fenêtre.

3

Voici Madame dans la maison.
Elle baisse le store.
Remarquez les rideaux.

CONTACT TEN FEELING UNWELL

Feeling unwell

Travel trouble

Travelling from one country to another affects some people. A change of climate, drinking water, food and daily routine can sometimes cause minor upsets. If you can explain to someone what the matter is, the chances are that you will feel a lot better straightaway. You are going to learn to say in French that you feel unwell, to explain where the pain is, and how bad it is.

Where it hurts

Here are some of the troubles you might have.

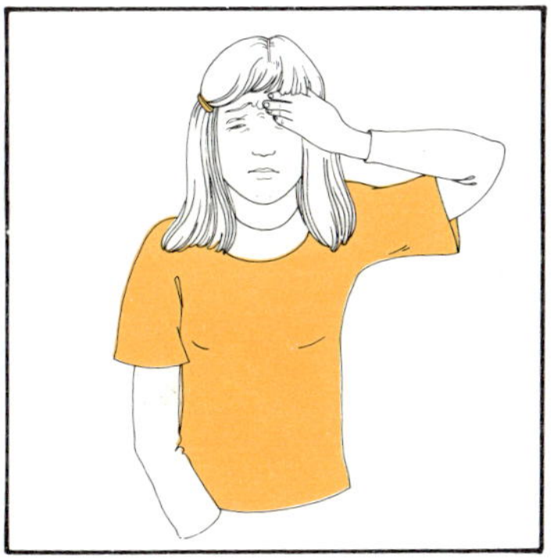

mal à la tête

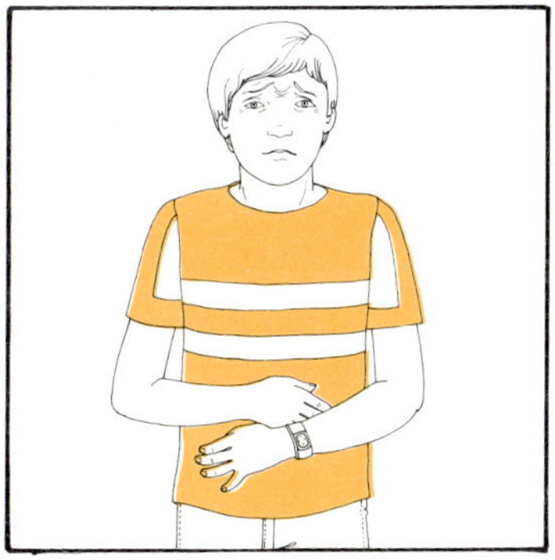

mal au ventre

mal aux oreilles

mal à la gorge

mal au cœur

mal aux dents

Model Dialogue 1

In this scene Angela has a headache, which is very bad. Yvette takes Angela off to look after her.

Model Dialogue 2

In this scene David has a stomach upset, which hurts a little. Lucien's father takes David away to look after him.

What was that question again?

Are you ill? **Tu es malade?**
Vous êtes malade?

What's the matter? **Qu'est-ce que tu as?**
Qu'est-ce que vous avez?
Qu'est-ce qu'il y a?
Qu'est-ce qui ne va pas?

Just Looking

You can easily understand how important it is to be able to read some of the details on the boxes and bottles that contain medicines. Taking too many tablets, or drinking something which ought to be rubbed on could have serious results. There are a few words and phrases which you really do need to be able to understand. Here is some practice for you.

1

These instructions are on a box containing a bottle of *Cortiphénicol* drops.

(a) What are the drops intended for?
(b) How many drops should you use at a time?
(c) How many times a day should you use the drops?
(d) Should you drink the drops?

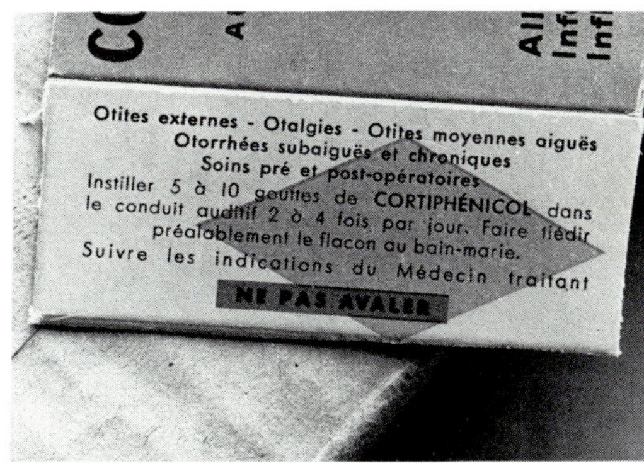

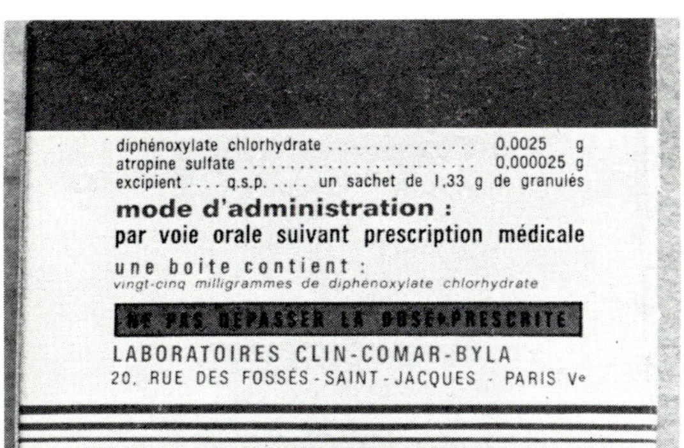

2

This box contains *Diarsed* for the treatment of upset stomachs.

(a) What do these instructions tell you about the quantity to take?
(b) What warning is printed on the box?

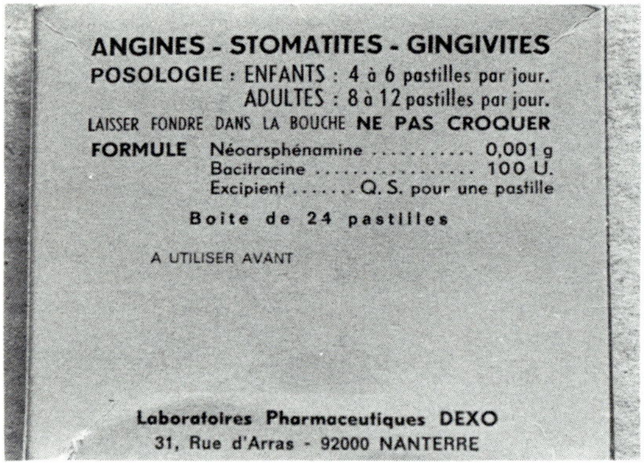

3

Here is a box of *Collunovar* pastilles.

(a) How should you take them?

(b) Would you take them for a sore throat, or for a stomach ache?

(c) What is the biggest number of pastilles that a child should take in one day?

4

This is a box of *Doliprane* tablets.

(a) How many tablets are there in a full box?

(b) Would you take these tablets if you had a temperature, ear-ache, the 'flu, an upset stomach, or tooth-ache?

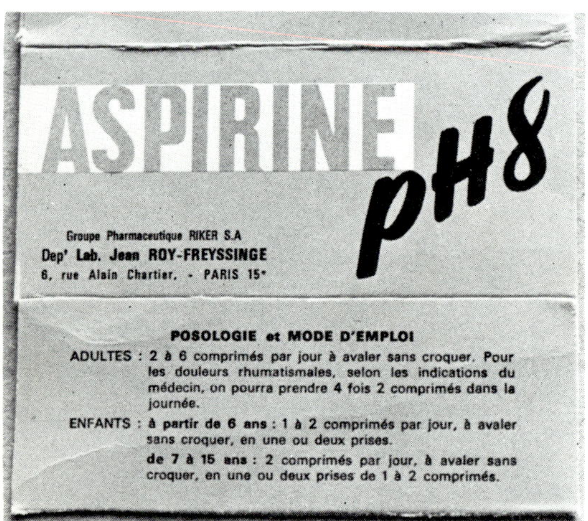

5

This box contains aspirin tablets.

(a) How many tablets per day are recommended for a 14 year old?

(b) How should you take them?

(c) How many are you allowed to take at a time?

Puzzle it out!

A conversation with a doctor in which you tell him how you feel, and he tells you what you must do to get better, could be quite difficult. Here is an example for you to puzzle out.

Ça ne va pas

Docteur: Alors, ça ne va pas très bien aujourd'hui?
Hazel: Oh, non ! Je suis malade, et j'ai chaud.
Docteur: Et vous avez mal?
Hazel: Oui, monsieur. J'ai mal à la tête et à la gorge.
Docteur: Ouvrez la bouche, s'il vous plaît.
Hazel: Aaah.
Docteur: Hmm, pas très joli, ça. Vous avez un peu de fièvre. C'est certainement la grippe. Les oreilles ne vous font pas mal?
Hazel: Non, monsieur.
Docteur: Tant mieux. Vous allez rester trois jours au lit, mademoiselle. Au bout des trois jours ça ira mieux. Il faut prendre de l'aspirine – quatre comprimés par jour – et des pastilles pour la gorge. Vous en laissez fondre une dans la bouche toutes les deux heures. Voici une ordonnance pour le pharmacien.
Hazel: Merci, monsieur le docteur.

1 How does Hazel feel exactly?
2 Where does she feel her aches and pains?
3 Has she got a temperature?
4 What does the doctor say is the matter with her?
5 How long must she stay in bed?
6 What does the doctor prescribe for Hazel?
7 What doses does he recommend?
8 How should Hazel take the second item prescribed?

That's not funny!

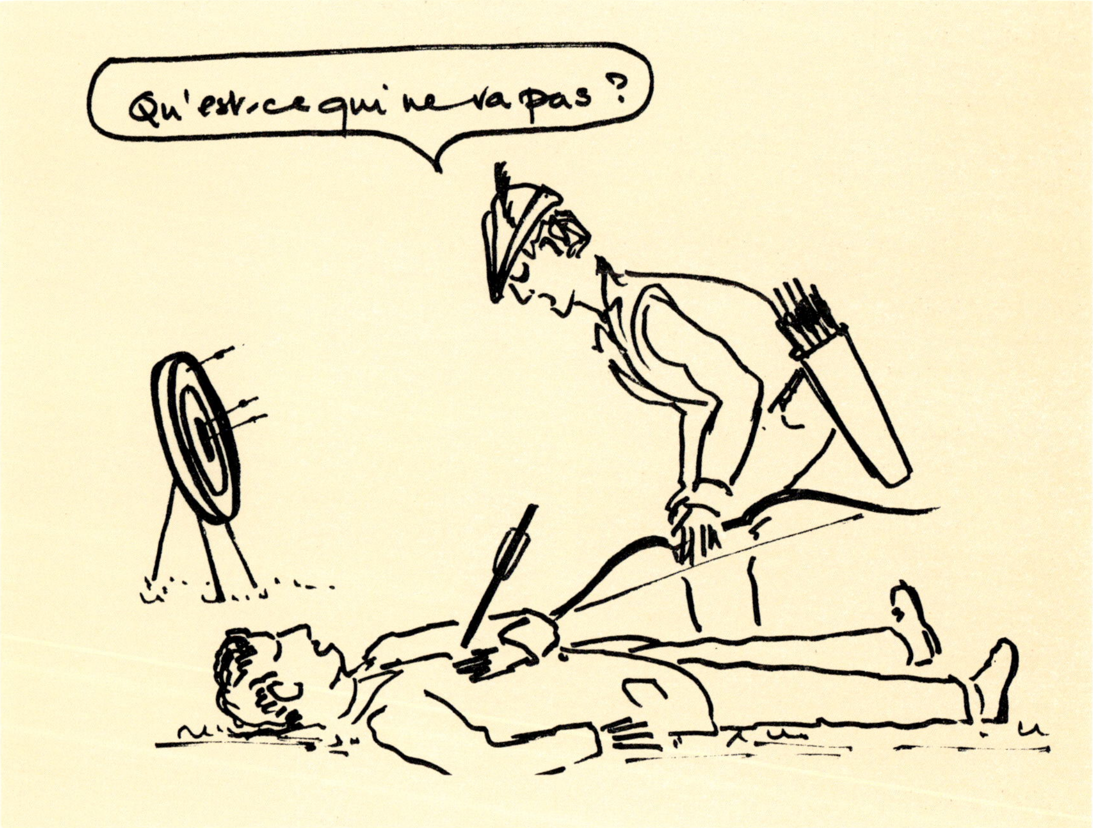

Let's write

(a) Imagine you have been feeling terrible and your friend's mother has sent for the doctor. You are not feeling at all confident about telling him how you feel, so you decide to write down some key phrases. Make a short list of the things you should say to the doctor.
(b) The doctor has come and given his instructions. You want to make sure that you remember them and that you can understand them. Write down some possible instructions.
It will help you if you look back at 'Puzzle it out!' and 'Just Looking'.

Looking round the House

La Poubelle

Voici la poubelle derrière la maison. Il y a aussi un seau. Entre la poubelle et le seau il y a un chat. Les chats aiment bien les poubelles.

1

2

SELECTED VOCABULARY

Meanings given suit the context. French words are arranged in alphabetical order within separate Contacts.

Contact 1

d'accord	in agreement
ainsi	so, thus
aujourd'hui	today
tu auras	you will have
chambre	bedroom
chez	at, to the house of
chez moi	at my house, with me
chez ma tante	to my aunt's
connaissance	acquaintance
copains	pals, friends, mates
je t'écris	I am writing to you
enfin	at last, finally
j'espère	I hope
tu feras	you will make
jours	days
partir	to go away
passer	to spend
pendant	during
quinze	fifteen
réponds	reply
vacances	holidays
les grandes vacances	summer holidays
venir	to come

Contact 2

baleine	whale
bière	beer
boivent	drink (they)
café	coffee
Camembert	the name of a French cheese
dauphine	a style of cooking potatoes

framboise	raspberry
légumes	vegetables
mer	sea
un peu	a little
me plaît	pleases me (= I like, enjoy)
pommes (de terre)	potatoes
potage	soup
poulet	chicken
raffiné	refined
Roquefort	the name of a French cheese
sel	salt
sucre	sugar
surchoix	finest quality
tartine	slice of bread
thé	tea
yaourt	yoghurt

Contact 3

bulles	bubbles
eau minérale	mineral water
écrémé	skim (milk)
gazeuse	gassy, fizzy
huile	oil
jus	juice
lait	milk
or	gold
raisin	grapes
sans	without

Contact 4

s'aplaniront	will smooth themselves out
astres	stars
vous aurez	you will have
avantage	
à votre avantage	at your best, looking your best
en banlieue	in the suburbs
connais	know
convaincre	to convince

donnera	will give
le droit	the right
vous dépenser	to push yourself
économe	economical
je m'ennuie	I'm bored
envie	
vous aurez envie	you will wish
d'eux-mêmes	of their own accord
fascinera	will fascinate
formidable	terrific, fantastic, smashing
gardez	keep
gens	people
n'hésitez pas	do not hesitate
histoire	story
incompréhension	lack of understanding
inébranlable	unshakeable
jamais	ever
plus que jamais	more than ever
journée	day
laisser	to let, allow
lucidité	lucidity, clear headedness
malheureuse	unhappy
même	same
quelqu'un	someone
rencontrer	to meet
résistance	stamina
réunion	meeting
rien à faire	nothing to do
rigolent	laugh
seule	alone, only
le soir	in the evening
soyez	be
tête froide	cool head
vraie	real, true

Contact 5

ajoutez	add
beurre	butter

bouillon concentré	stock
bouteille	bottle
chaud	hot
citron	lemon
cocotte	stew-pan
un coup de main	a (helping) hand
cuillerée	spoonful
cuisson	cooking
échalote	shallot
glaçons	ice-cubes
huile	oil
lapereau	young rabbit
lapin	rabbit
librairie	bookshop
mécano	mechanic
ménagère	housewife
mettez	put
montagnes	mountains
persil	parsely
plat de service	serving dish
poivre	pepper
saupoudrez	sprinkle
sel	salt
tablette	cube
tranche	slice
travaillent	work
vendeuse	shop assistant
verre	glass
versez	pour
volaille	poultry

Contact 6

allemand	German
nous avons	we have
beaucoup	a lot
bilan	facts and figures, balance of account
chimie	chemistry
concours	competitions
courses	races

dédoublée	setted (class, on timetable)
dessin	drawing, art
disques	records
EPS = Education Physique et Sports	
équipes	teams
espoirs	hopes
grammaire	grammar
hippiques	equestrian, horse
hippodrome	race-course (horses)
instruction civique	civics
tu joues	you play
lecture	reading
lecture expliquée	critical analysis of short extracts from French literature
lecture suivie	study of whole works of French literature
natation	swimming
nordistes	northerners
orthographe	spelling
patins à roulettes	roller-skates, -skating
perdre	to lose
permanence	supervised private study
un risque	a risk
sciences naturelles	natural sciences, biology
sévère	strict
technologie	engineering science, physics
travaux manuels	handicraft
3^{e}	3rd
je trouve	I find

Contact 7

actualités	current events
allemand	German
anglais	English
boxe	boxing
émissions	broadcasts
étranger	foreign
flèche	arrow
en flèche	like an arrow, very fast (spreading)
glace	ice
janvier	January

jeunesse	youth, young people
jusqu'à	until
à quoi bon . . . ?	what is the use of . . .?
semaine	week
tir à l'arc	archery

Contact 8

achats	purchases
faire les achats	to do the shopping
Bruxelles	Brussels
chambre	bedroom
dim. = dimanche	Sunday
gens	people
jeu. = jeudi	Thursday
mat. = matinée	afternoon performance
mauvais	bad
il fait mauvais	the weather is bad
noir et blanc	black and white
pêche	fishing
places	seats
tu le sais	you know
séjour	stay
sf. = sauf	except
t.l.s. = tous les soirs	every evening
en vélo	by bike
v.f. = version française	French version (of sound track)
v.o. = version originale	original version (of sound track)

Contact 9

ailleurs	elsewhere
amélioration	improvement
basses	low
beau	fine
il fait beau	the weather is fine
brouillard	fog
brumeux	misty
chutes	falls

ciel	sky
cœur	heart
courrier	letters, post
courses	racing, races
couvert	overcast (sky)
cuisine	cookery
éclaircies	clear periods
étranger	foreign
faible	light, weak
gelée	frost
givrant	freezing
intéressant	interesting
au lever du jour	at dawn
livres	books
marché	market
matinales	morning, in the morning
météorologie	meteorology, weather forecast
mots-croisés	crosswords
neige	snow
nord	north
nuageux	cloudy
partie	part
pays	country
pluie	rain
la poste	post office
rester	to stay
sommaire	summary
spectacles	shows (theatre, cinema)
vent	wind
voyage	travel, journey

Contact 10

angine	tonsillitis
avaler	swallow
bouche	mouth
comprimés	tablets
croquer	to crunch, munch
dépasser	to exceed, go past
douleurs	pains

fièvre	fever, high temperature
fois	times
fondre	to melt, dissolve
gingivites	gingivitis, infection of gums
gouttes	drops
laisser	allow, let
médecin	doctor
mode	way, manner
mode d'emploi	directions, instructions
otalgies	ear-aches
otites	ear infections
par	per
par jour	per day
à partir de	from
posologie	quantity of medicines to be taken
prescrite	prescribed
prise	action of taking
stomatites	inflammation of the mouth
suivant	according to, in accordance with
tiédir	
faire tiédir	warm
par voie orale	orally, through the mouth